RUDY'S LESSONS FOR YOUNG CHAMPIONS

Rudy's Lessons for Young Champions:

CHOICES AND CHALLENGES

by
RUDY & CHERYL RUETTIGER
BILL & REBECCA WOLFE ATKINSON

Illustrated by
Rebecca Wolfe Atkinson

RUDY INTERNATIONAL PUBLICATIONS LTD.
Henderson, Nevada 89014

First printed in 1997
by Rudy International Publications LTD.
Henderson, Nevada 89014

Art work and illustrations
by Rebecca Wolfe Atkinson

Cover design and book layout
by Dennis Cooper

ISBN # 0-9658119-0-5
Library of Congress # 97-91934

This book is dedicated to all who have the courage to pursue their Dreams . . .
            —Rudy and Cheryl Ruettiger

Dedicated to my Creator for allowing me to be His pencil . . . and to my daughters, Rachel and Autumn, who endured countless eagle and crow lectures.
            —Bill and Rebecca Wolfe Atkinson

Table Of Contents

RUDY'S 12 LESSONS
FOR YOUNG CHAMPIONS

RUDY'S 12 LESSONS FOR YOUNG CHAMPIONS can be found at the end of each chapter. The lessons that relate most to that chapter will be highlighted. The idea is to help young people become very familiar with these Lessons, understand them, and learn to apply them to their lives everyday.

- Chapter 1 -
Rudy's Arrival

High above the tree line, on the western edge of Majestic Mountain, sat an eagle's nest. It was a beautiful nest, strong and well-protected from the winter wind and high above any danger. Within the nest were two newly hatched eaglets and one still unhatched egg.

The two eaglets had been out of their eggs for almost two days. They were strong and always hungry. This kept their parents busy filling their hungry bellies.

Mother Eagle was worried about her unhatched third egg. She knew that if it didn't hatch soon, she would have to throw it out to make room for her two rapidly growing eaglets.

Inside the egg, a tiny eaglet struggled. He kicked and pushed until finally a tiny crack emerged. Then he pushed and pushed some more. "Such a strong shell," he thought.

Then, with all his might, he gave a giant PUSH.

Out popped his head. The sun was bright, and the sunlight almost blinded him.

When his eyes adjusted to the brightness, the first sights he saw were the wide-open mouths of his brothers and his mother stuffing food down their throats.

Barely out of his egg, he, too, was very hungry. He opened his mouth to be fed, but his brothers kept getting the food faster.

Life in an eagle's nest is first come, first served. Mealtime would be a struggle for this smallest of eaglets. His brothers, besides being older, were also more thoughtless and very greedy eaters. They couldn't care less whether their younger brother got fed.

Finally, Mother Eagle turned to her smallest eaglet.

She said, "Welcome, my little one. Boys, your brother is finally here." They never looked up from their food. "BOYS! BOYS!" she shouted, "let your little brother eat. He, too, needs food to grow. If you two keep hogging it all, he won't get any."

She then stuffed a delicious, fresh morsel of food into his mouth.

"How does that taste?" she asked. "Here, eat some more." She stuffed more food into her baby eaglet's mouth. "That will help you to grow and catch up with your brothers."

"You need a name, my little one," she said. "I know, your name will be RUDY. That is right. RUDY is a special name. Now you say it," she smiled.

Rudy beamed proudly as he chirped his first word,

"RU-UD-DY."

Then he said it again, "RU-DY." He said it a third time, "RUDY. What does it mean?" asked Rudy.

Rudy's mother said, "Your name means *To Inspire*."

"What does inspire mean, Mother?" Rudy asked. "It means to be a good example for others and never quit," replied Mother.

Rudy gave her a big smile and said, "Mother, I like my name. I like what it means."

Rudy had arrived.

Discussion Questions

1. Why does Rudy like his name?

2. Struggle means to work really hard at something and to never quit, even when it gets tough. When you struggle you learn great life lessons. How does Rudy struggle in Chapter 1?

3. What does inspire mean?

4. Describe a time when you were inspired. What did it feel like?

RUDY'S 12 LESSONS FOR YOUNG CHAMPIONS

1. Develop your Dream and set realistic goals.

2. Get advice and good information from mentors who believe in your Dream.

3. Listen to good positive music, read positive books, and watch positive movies.

4. Hang out with friends that encourage you, not friends that put you down.

5. Always be a good example for others.

6. Inspire others to be their best.

7. Believe in yourself and take action. Action eliminates fear.

8. Prepare for your Dream, focus, and achieve your goals step by step.

9. Use anger in a positive way, to help you overcome your struggles and do something good.

10. Develop courage, faith, and wisdom and go for your Dream.

11. Have a "YES I CAN" attitude.

12. Never Quit!

- Chapter 2 -
Rudy and the Beginning of the Dream

"Mother," Rudy asked, "why is Rudy a special name?"

"All my eaglets have special names. But you, Rudy, are named after my father. Rudy was your grandeagle's name. He, too, was late in hatching and small, but he grew to be a great WIND DANCER. It is a mother and father eagle's Dream that all their eaglets grow to be Wind Dancers," she answered.

"What is a Wind Dancer, Mother?" asked Rudy.

"Yes . . . tell us, Mother," shouted the other two eaglets.

Mother explained to her eaglets, "Well, all eagles have the gift of flight. A Wind Dancer has a special gift, a spirit of challenge, that comes from deep, deep inside the heart. All creatures have a special purpose in life. An eagle's special purpose is to become a Wind Dancer. Eagles know this purpose very soon. They feel it deep inside. However, not all eagles have the courage to become a Wind Dancer."

She continued and pointed to the sky. "Above the clouds, the mountain currents are very strong. Only Wind Dancers can survive the currents. They can soar and dance with the highest and strongest mountain winds because they know where they are going. Wind Dancers belong to the sky. It is truly a beautiful and inspirational sight to behold," said the mother.

"I will be a Wind Dancer," shouted one of the nestlings.

"Me too," shouted the other one, even louder.

Rudy thought, "I was named after my grandeagle, a great Wind Dancer. I am a Wind Dancer."

That night Rudy dreamed of soaring high above the earth, where other birds don't dare to fly.

The Dream was now set in Rudy's mind.

Discussion Questions

1. What is a Dream?

2. Rudy's Dream is to become a Wind Dancer. Do you have a Dream?

3. Describe your Dream and how it makes you feel.

4. The story of Rudy's grandeagle inspired Rudy to Dream about becoming a Wind Dancer. If you have a Dream, what or who inspired your Dream?

5. If you don't have a Dream, let's develop one. Use your imagination. What have you always wanted to do or become? What makes you happy?

6. Why is it important to have a Dream?

RUDY'S 12 LESSONS FOR YOUNG CHAMPIONS

1. Develop your Dream and set realistic goals.

2. Get advice and good information from mentors who believe in your Dream.

3. Listen to good positive music, read positive books, and watch positive movies.

4. Hang out with friends that encourage you, not friends that put you down.

5. Always be a good example for others.

6. Inspire others to be their best.

7. Believe in yourself and take action. Action eliminates fear.

8. Prepare for your Dream, focus, and achieve your goals step by step.

9. Use anger in a positive way, to help you overcome your struggles and do something good.

10. Develop courage, faith, and wisdom and go for your Dream.

11. Have a "YES I CAN" attitude.

12. Never Quit!

- Chapter 3 -
Rudy and Mother's Wind Dancer
Tale

Rudy awoke the next morning feeling excited, restless, and enthusiastic. All night long he had thought that he was a Wind Dancer. Yet, when he woke in the morning, Rudy realized that he had only been dreaming.

He turned to his mother and asked, "Mother, how does one become a Wind Dancer?"

Mother stopped feeding Rudy's brothers. "Are you hungry, Rudy?" she asked. "You must be hungry. Look how hungry your brothers are. You better eat, Rudy!"

"Mother," Rudy responded, "I can't eat. I dreamt all night about being a Wind Dancer! I have to know more about wind dancing."

Rudy's two brothers shouted together, "Mother, Mother, please tell us more about becoming a Wind Dancer."

Mother now realized that her sons would
need to know the full story of their grandeagle and how he became a Wind Dancer.

"Sit back my eaglets," Mother said, "I will
tell you the Wind Dancer tale."

Mother begins the tale.

Many seasons ago, before my birth, when your grandeagle was very young, there was only one Wind Dancer left among the eagles. This Wind Dancer was quite old, and after his passing there would be no surviving Wind Dancer to pass on the ancient secrets of the mountain currents. Of course, all the young eagles were working very hard to achieve the honor of becoming a Wind Dancer.

There was great excitement among the eagles, and all of the forest creatures, as to which eagle would earn the honor. There was also an underlying sadness among all the creatures. No one would speak of it, but many thought it. What would happen if no eagle had the courage to learn the secret of the winds and become a Wind Dancer? The secret would then return to the winds. No one wanted to mention that possibility.

Remember, my sons, your grandeagle was small. He was also very young and un-worldly. Few, if any, took notice of him. What no one could see was the enormous vision of his Dream and the size of his heart. He was an eagle. He had the eagle spirit, the eagle heart, and the Dream to become a Wind Dancer.

Unfortunately, many of the other eagles tried to discourage him from even trying to become a Wind Dancer. They told him he was too small, too inexperienced, and too unknowledgeable about the way of the winds. They said that his wings could never weather such currents. Even his friends in the woods kept telling him that he could not achieve his Dream.

At times, he even began to doubt that he could become a Wind Dancer.

"Can I really fly with the winds?" he wondered.

As I told you, my father, your grandeagle was very small, but inside he carried the seed of greatness.

 That season, long ago, "Ole Man Winter" came early. Winter came from the north with surprisingly savage force and caught all of the forest creatures un-

aware. For days, sheets of ice and rain beat against the mountain.

The eagles had prepared for the Wind Dancers' ceremony in hope that one of the young eagles would have the courage to achieve their life's purpose. Any eagle could achieve the ancient secrets of the mountain currents. The secret is in all eagles. It is there for those who are willing to learn and accept the challenge.

The winds were too violent, that season, for even the most skilled and strongest of eagles. They all clung to their nests and waited for the weather to pass. But, the weather and the wind became the worst ever. It grew so strong that it sounded like the roar of a lion. Many began to fear for their very lives.

Suddenly, from above the roaring wind, the eagles heard a "SCHREECCHH." Within the violent storm flew the old Wind Dancer. He knew that his days were getting fewer and fewer. But, he was a Wind Dancer. It would be a contest between nature's worst and the old Wind Dancer's skills.

The wind howled and roared in an attempt to dash the old Wind Dancer into the cliffs. Still, the old Wind Dancer continued to dance, dodge, and soar with the wind. All the eagles and the animals of the forest watched in awe as the old Wind Dancer took control of the wind. He made this most monstrous of storms appear no more dangerous than a gentle summer's breeze.

The old Wind Dancer had challenged the storm and was able to control its rage and anger. He now flew higher and higher, circling the canyon. As he rose, he appeared more beautiful and more powerful than any had seen him before.

Then, the old Wind Dancer cried out to all the eagles, "My time is growing short. It is our belief that all living things have been placed here for a special purpose. It is an eagle's purpose to become a Wind Dancer. This honor is not just for one eagle, but for all eagles. Yet, only a few will have the heart to achieve their purpose in life. This is an honor which is achievable by all eagles who develop the courage, faith, wisdom, and the knowledge to survive the struggle with the wind."

He paused and waited. Then he said, "If none has the heart, the vision, or the passion to learn the secret of flying with the winds, then upon my passing the ancient secret will

be released back to the wind. The secret will be lost forever."

"Lost forever, Mother?" gasped Rudy.

"Yes. LOST FOREVER!" Mother continued.

Of course, all the eagles trembled with fear at the thought that the secret of the Wind Dancer would be lost forever.

The old Wind Dancer continued to wait, but his time was running out. He sadly began to fold his wings and give himself to the storm. He would, then, rejoin the Creator.

It would have been a tragic day for all eagles if your grandeagle, Rudy, had not willingly dove into the violent storm to face the wind. All the other eagles were unable to move. They just watched. They were certain that he would be killed by the storm.

Your grandeagle fought the storm and struggled to catch up with the old Wind Dancer. The storm wanted the ancient secrets back, but your grandeagle had prepared and was very focused. Whatever the storm threw at him, he threw it back. He was determined to catch up with the old Wind Dancer and save the secret of the wind currents. He was an eagle. It was his purpose in life to become a Wind Dancer.

It seemed an endless struggle, but your grandeagle never gave up. Finally, he flew beside the old Wind Dancer. He looked at your grandeagle, and he was pleased. He could see Rudy's courage, and he honored his struggle.

"The secrets of Wind Dancing lie within each of us, brave one," the old Wind Dancer said. "It is the courage and heart to endure the struggle that gives us such wisdom. Few have such courage, but all creatures possess a seed of greatness."

His work completed, he rose higher and higher. He was now ready to return to the Creator.

Your grandeagle, Rudy, watched as the old Wind Dancer became one with the sky, mountains, and the winds. He, like the old Wind Dancers before him, could now dodge, soar, and dance with the wind as if the storm was only a gentle summer's breeze. He was a Wind Dancer. He was now the greatest of eagles.

Discussion Questions

1. What did Rudy's grandeagle have to develop to achieve his Dream of becoming a Wind Dancer?

2. What Struggles did the grandeagle face? What did he learn?

3. What is courage? Discuss a time when you felt courage. What did you do? What did you learn?

4. Why didn't the other eagles become Wind Dancers?

RUDY'S 12 LESSONS FOR YOUNG CHAMPIONS

1. Develop your Dream and set realistic goals.

2. Get advice and good information from mentors who believe in your Dream.

3. Listen to good positive music, read positive books, and watch positive movies.

4. Hang out with friends that encourage you, not friends that put you down.

5. Always be a good example for others.

6. Inspire others to be their best.

7. Believe in yourself and take action. Action eliminates fear.

8. Prepare for your Dream, focus, and achieve your goals step by step.

9. Use anger in a positive way, to help you overcome your struggles and do something good.

10. Develop courage, faith, and wisdom and go for your Dream.

11. Have a "YES I CAN" attitude.

12. Never Quit!

- Chapter 4 -
Rudy Forgets the Dream

One afternoon, Rudy was alone in the nest, waiting for his mother to return. Rudy had been anxious to fly. His brothers, who were much bigger than him, had been flying for several days now.

Below his nest Rudy heard much commotion. He looked over the side of the nest. Far below flew a flock of crows. From where Rudy watched, they looked like a dark cloud of wings. They created so much noise. Rudy leaned farther out from his nest to get a better look. He had never seen so many birds before or had heard such a ruckus. He continued to stretch farther and farther out from his nest until suddenly there was no nest beneath him, only air!

"Fly! Fly! Fly!" he yelled.

Frantically, Rudy flapped his young, tiny, little wings. He spread his pin feathers to catch the wind, just like he had seen his parents do so many times. But, instead of going up, he continued to tumble down toward the tree line far below.

He crashed with a thud.

Rudy felt a sharp pain in his right wing. When he opened his eyes, he was beak-to-beak with two newly-hatched crows.

"AAHHH!" he screamed, holding his injured wing.

"CAAAAWWWWW!" screamed the baby crows.

They thought Rudy was their *giant*, newly hatched brother.

"I'm Kackle," said the smaller of the two crows. He spoke with a lisp and had a way of spitting as he talked. He was a friendly sort of bird.

The other crow was not as friendly or welcoming to Rudy's arrival. Instead, he glared at Rudy with suspicion. This crow then took off his red headband and blew his nose rather loudly into it. To Rudy's disgust, he tied it back on his head.

This crow opened his mouth, as if to speak, but instead he broke into a fit of

coughing, snorting, and spitting up great gobs of snot.

"That's Hacker. He's allergic to feathers," giggled Kackle.

"I'm Rudy," he proudly announced. "I am named after my grandeagle, a famous Wind Dancer. My name means *To Inspire*."

"Sssshhh! Crows don't speak about such things," Kackle warned.

"Wind Dancer! Wind Dancer! Wind Dancer! Such nonsense," shrieked Hacker. "Where are your crow colors?"

The crow brothers pointed out their red headbands, as they checked out Rudy.

"I don't know," Rudy answered, still holding his hurt wing.

"What's ya got? . . . a bum wing?" asked Kackle.

"It hurts when I try to stretch it out," Rudy said making a face that showed pain as he tried to extend his wing.

"Then don't stretch it, STUPID!" chuck-led Hacker through his hacking cough.

"How will I ever be able to fly if I can't extend my wing?" cried Rudy.

"That's the beauty of being a crow! All we do is flutter and hop around the tree line. No aerial acrobatics for us. Nope. None of that crazy stuff," Hacker coughed.

Kackle added, "Take it easy, brother! There is no need to stretch out that wing. Us crows know how to live the life of lei-sure."

"Of course, if you want to get fed," Kackle said, "then you had better talk crow and put on your colors."

Kackle tied crow colors on Rudy's head. He was delighted to have such a large brother, but Hacker continued to remain suspicious of Rudy.

So, Rudy tightly tucked in his wing and kept his Dream about becoming a Wind Dancer to himself.

Discussion Questions

1. Why did Rudy decide to keep his Dream to himself? How did he feel?

2. The crows advised Rudy that in order to be accepted by the crows, he better act like the crows . . . that meant not trying to stretch-out his wing. If Rudy follows the crows' advice, will he be able to become a Wind Dancer?

3. When Rudy was around the crows he felt like he couldn't be himself. Describe a time when you felt like you couldn't be yourself? How did you feel? What did you do about it? Did you feel like maybe you were in the wrong situation? or like you were with the wrong people?

RUDY'S 12 LESSONS FOR YOUNG CHAMPIONS

1. Develop your Dream and set realistic goals.

2. Get advice and good information from mentors who believe in your Dream.

3. Listen to good positive music, read positive books, and watch positive movies.

4. Hang out with friends that encourage you, not friends that put you down.

5. Always be a good example for others.

6. Inspire others to be their best.

7. Believe in yourself and take action. Action eliminates fear.

8. Prepare for your Dream, focus, and achieve your goals step by step.

9. Use anger in a positive way, to help you overcome your struggles and do something good.

10. Develop courage, faith, and wisdom and go for your Dream.

11. Have a "YES I CAN" attitude.

12. Never Quit!

- *Chapter 5* -
Rudy Becomes Confused

Mother Eagle returned to the nest to find Rudy missing. She prayed that he had learned to fly and was out with his brothers. But, Rudy's pinfeathers were still so small. Frantic with worry, she searched for her future Wind Dancers. Mother Eagle searched all the places that a baby eagle would be able to fly. Soaring high above the canyons, cliffs, and mountains, she finally spotted two of her sons. They were perched on a high cliff above Monarch Canyon studying the wind. There was no sign of Rudy.

"Have you seen your brother, Rudy?" Mother Eagle called out to her sons.

"He's not with us Mother. Rudy was in the nest when we left to go flying," explained her young eagles.

"The nest is empty. He must be around somewhere. You boys get back home in case Rudy returns, and I'll keep looking for him," said Mother with a hopeful voice.

Rudy's Mother knew that an eaglet of Rudy's age and size would have a difficult time feeding himself. He still needed his mother and the protection of the nest. Her search went on for days. Still, there was no sign of Rudy. Mother returned to the nest, but not a day went by that she didn't look for her missing son. Mother Eagle knew that she would never give up searching for her missing boy, but she also knew that she had two other sons who needed her love and attention. She must not forget about them . . . there was still a lot that she needed to teach them.

But far down below the high cliffs and mountain tops, where eagles don't usually fly, there was Rudy. Rudy had changed. Instead of thinking about becoming a great Wind Dancer like his grandeagle, he made himself believe that he was a crow. It was easier to blend in with the crows than to Dream.

The crows loved to eat garbage. To eat with the crows Rudy had to hold his nose. They ate the most disgusting and foul-smelling trash. He really wanted to eat the fresh, wholesome food that his mother had fed to him. How he missed his mother and

his two brothers. But he had to forget about them and his Dreams if he wanted to fit in.

Even when flying, he never tried to extend his injured wing fully. In fact, by now it had healed and was very strong. But Rudy wanted to fit in.

Besides, he had a new gang of friends. They were not eagles. They were crows. Crows don't play with eagles. Crows don't even like eagles.

Since falling and injuring his wing, Rudy had become afraid to fly. The idea of flying high or fast was now scary even to Rudy.

So Rudy fluttered around the tree line with jerky, frantic wing movements. Even though it felt awkward to fly like that, Rudy wanted so badly to fit in with the crows that he soon forgot all about being an eagle.

Discussion Questions

1. Why did Rudy forget about being an eagle and decide to hang out with the crows?

2. What made Rudy feel different than his crow friends? In what ways did Rudy think differently than his crow friends?

3. What is peer pressure?

4. Is it easier to try to "fit in" or to be ourselves? Is it better to be ourselves, even if that is different from our friends, if we are doing the right things? Why?

RUDY'S 12 LESSONS FOR YOUNG CHAMPIONS

1. Develop your Dream and set realistic goals.

2. Get advice and good information from mentors who believe in your Dream.

3. Listen to good positive music, read positive books, and watch positive movies.

4. Hang out with friends that encourage you, not friends that put you down.

5. Always be a good example for others.

6. Inspire others to be their best.

7. Believe in yourself and take action. Action eliminates fear.

8. Prepare for your Dream, focus, and achieve your goals step by step.

9. Use anger in a positive way, to help you overcome your struggles and do something good.

10. Develop courage, faith, and wisdom and go for your Dream.

11. Have a "YES I CAN" attitude.

12. Never Quit!

- Chapter 6 -
Rudy Tries to Fit In

At first it was easy to fit in, because eaglets are born all one color. But, as Rudy grew, his head and tail feathers began to change. He quickly learned to hide them. He thought that it would be safer to look like a crow.

The crows dressed, spoke, and acted alike. Crows only flew with other crows. If other birds or forest animals came near, the crows would make fun of them and would drive them away.

"Let's chase and peck Ole Mr. Groundhog. He's old and fat!" teased one of the crows.

They all agreed.

"Let's go and dive bomb some robin nests!" spoke another crow.

Rudy thought the games were cruel, but he knew better than to say anything. He enjoyed the different birds and other forest animals. In fact, he liked Mr. Groundhog. Rudy had met him briefly one day down by the river.

Rudy flew down to see Mr. Groundhog.

Mr. Groundhog was sweeping the path to his burrow.

"I'm always tidying up . . . YUP, YUP . . . I like it neat . . . I do," Mr. Groundhog said as he poked at Rudy's feet with his broom.

"Off my path!" Mr. Groundhog yelled.

Rudy quickly moved to one side.

"Mr. Groundhog, it's me, Rudy!" Rudy reminded.

"Young Rudy, YUP, YUP . . . a young Rudy bird," Mr. Groundhog chuckled.

"What kind of bird are you, young Rudy?" Mr. Groundhog asked.

"Ah . . . Ah . . . Ah . . . A CROW," Rudy replied.

Mr. Groundhog frowned. "Those crows are messy and rude. They're always pecking at me and thinkin' their teasing's funny . . . YUP, YUP. Suppose you'll be dropping your tail feathers all over the place."

Mr. Groundhog took a closer look at Rudy.

"What makes you think you're a crow?" he asked.

"My crow friends said so. See my crow colors," said Rudy pointing to his head-band.

"Seems a bit TIGHT . . . could be cutting off the blood supply to your brain . . . young Rudy," Mr. Groundhog said.

Mr. Groundhog put his eye specks on for a closer look. "You're still small and . . . kind of hard to tell yet . . ." he said.

He poked at Rudy's thick chest. "YUP, YUP . . . young Rudy . . . could be . . . you could be . . ." Mr. Groundhog took a close look at Rudy, "YUP, YUP . . . an eagle bird!"

Discussion Questions

1. What are the characteristics of a crow? Do crows have Dreams?

2. The crows felt good by teasing and putting others down. Are the crows a good example for us to follow? If we become like the crows, will we be able to live our Dreams? Why or Why not?

3. Yupper didn't like the way the crows acted. Why?

RUDY'S 12 LESSONS FOR YOUNG CHAMPIONS

1. Develop your Dream and set realistic goals.

2. Get advice and good information from mentors who believe in your Dream.

3. Listen to good positive music, read positive books, and watch positive movies.

4. Hang out with friends that encourage you, not friends that put you down.

5. Always be a good example for others.

6. Inspire others to be their best.

7. Believe in yourself and take action. Action eliminates fear.

8. Prepare for your Dream, focus, and achieve your goals step by step.

9. Use anger in a positive way, to help you overcome your struggles and do something good.

10. Develop courage, faith, and wisdom and go for your Dream.

11. Have a "YES I CAN" attitude.

12. Never Quit!

- Chapter 7 -
Rudy and Yupper's Discovery

Rudy protested, "I'm not. I'm not an eagle. My friends told me I'm a crow."

It had been so long. He was truly confused about who he was.

"Those friends never looked under that too tight headband! YUP, YUP . . . an eagle," Mr. Groundhog said rocking back on his heels, proud of his discovery.

"If you're a crow, you can call me Mr. Groundhog . . . Sir! But, if you're an eagle, call me Yupper," he said.

"An eagle?" Rudy thought to himself.

He tried to picture himself soaring with the wind currents. He had grown accustomed to flying with his hurt wing tucked in. It would be painful to fly with it extended, he told himself.

Rudy continued to convince himself that he was a crow. He thought that it felt good to be accepted and to belong to a group.

Besides, his crow friends were small and had no Dreams of flying above the tree line. It was easy for Rudy not to pursue his Dream when he was with the crows. He didn't have to work that hard. Also, his crow friends cared about him. Didn't they?

He thought back to what the crows had told him. "Hey Rudy, eat some garbage dude . . . be like us. Dress like us. Be cool! Don't fly too high, Rudy. You are not an eagle, you know," they would tell him.

Rudy remembered, all too well, what it was like to fall from a high place. "But," he thought, "if I am an eagle, I have to fly high. I have to soar with the strong mountain wind currents."

What once had excited Rudy now scared him.

He looked at Yupper and said, "I CAN'T! I hurt my wing and I can't extend it."

Yupper shook his head. "You can't or you won't! Rudy bird, you've gotten used to flying all bound up like a crow. They're a CAN'T kind of bird!" he scolded.

Yupper continued, "Change is painful. But you won't grow if you ain't willing to change."

"Rudy," Yupper said, "eagles hate that word . . . CAN'T!"

"Dag nabit, I hate *Canters* . . . Can't do this, Can't do that . . . most *Canters* ain't never even tried. Don't be thinkin' Can't, Rudy, think YES I CAN! Now, you, say it!" said Yupper.

"Yes I can," whispered Rudy, shyly.

"Stronger Rudy . . . YES I CAN!" shouted the old groundhog.

"Gosh, Mr. Groundhog . . . Sir, I . . . I mean Yupper. How will I know if I have what it takes to be an eagle?" Rudy asked.

"Time, young Rudy, . . . YUP, YUP . . . time," continued Yupper. "You need to get off by yourself, away from those noisy crows. It's hard to think straight with those crows all around . . . YUP, YUP. That's what you need to do. Those crows say you're a crow . . . YUP, YUP. Well, I say you're an eagle bird."

Yupper scratched his head. Then he said, "Yupper could be wrong . . . but . . . Yupper ain't been yet."

"Now what are you going to say instead of CAN'T?"

Yupper asked.

"YES I CAN!" exclaimed Rudy.

"You got it," cheered Yupper with pride and admiration for his young friend.

Smiling and happy inside, Yupper then scurried off to finish his tidying up.

As Rudy watched Yupper leave, he thought, "Yes I Can."

"YES I CAN."
　"YES I CAN."
　　"YES I CAN."
　　　"YES I CAN!" Rudy yelled out.

Discussion Questions

1. Yupper discovered that Rudy had the potential to be a great eagle. How did that change the way Rudy felt about himself?

2. What does Yupper teach Rudy? How is Yupper a good influence for Rudy?

3. A mentor is a good example and is a positive influence. It is someone that is looked up to, like a hero. Why are mentors important and how can they help you?

4. Describe what you will do when you are around *Canters* who put you down and say you can't live your Dreams. How will you think? What will you say?

RUDY'S 12 LESSONS FOR YOUNG CHAMPIONS

1. Develop your Dream and set realistic goals.

2. Get advice and good information from mentors who believe in your Dream.

3. Listen to good positive music, read positive books, and watch positive movies.

4. Hang out with friends that encourage you, not friends that put you down.

5. Always be a good example for others.

6. Inspire others to be their best.

7. Believe in yourself and take action. Action eliminates fear.

8. Prepare for your Dream, focus, and achieve your goals step by step.

9. Use anger in a positive way, to help you overcome your struggles and do something good.

10. Develop courage, faith, and wisdom and go for your Dream.

11. Have a "YES I CAN" attitude.

12. Never Quit!

- Chapter 8 -
Rudy Seeks to Learn the Truth

When Rudy returned to the tree line, he was confused, but his crow friends didn't notice. They were busy planning a garbage raid. Kackle and the gang were practicing their caws and squawks. It was giving Rudy a whopper of a headache.

"Give us a CAAWWWW, Rudy!" Kackle yelled when he saw Rudy.

"Maybe later, guys," Rudy replied.

"Come on, Rudy, CAAWWWW . . . you can't be a crow unless you sound like us," yelled another crow.

Cawing was the one thing that Rudy could not master. Every time he tried, the crows would look at him with suspicion. Several even laughed at his attempts.

A couple of crows asked Rudy, "What kind of crow couldn't or wouldn't caw?"

"Come on, Rudy, CAAWWWW," ordered his friends.

Rudy opened his great beak. "SCREECCCHHH," was the sound they all heard.

The flock grew silent.

Kackle, behaving quite uncrow-like, quickly went to Rudy's defense. "That Rudy, he thinks he's an eagle. Ha! Ha!" Kackle giggled. "Crazy Rudy. A crow trying to be an eagle."

"Come on, dude, . . . try to caw . . . be like us . . . be like us," the crows chanted.

The crows gathered around Rudy. They looked angry. All seemed angry except for Kackle. He was desperately trying to cover up for his nest mate.

"Come on, Rudy, . . . quit goofing around. He's teasing guys. Really . . . he's great at cawing . . . really," Kackle tried to convince the other crows.

Kackle turned and whispered to Rudy, "Caw, dude, or else your goose is cooked."

Rudy swallowed hard. He didn't feel like cawing. He felt like SCREEECCHHING.

He shut his eyes and thought about cawing, but when he opened his mouth, again, no sound came out.

"You'll sit this raid out, Mr. Eagle-Wanna-Be," the crows, except for Kackle, agreed.

"Maybe you'll feel like cawing when you're a bit hungrier." The crow flock turned and left.

Kackle turned to Rudy and asked, "What's wrong with you? Don't you want to be part of the gang?"

"I don't know, Kackle," Rudy answered. "You guys say that I am a crow, but inside I feel like I am . . ." Rudy paused.

Kackle put his wings over his ears and said, "Don't say it. Shuuusssssssh. Someone will hear you and know what you're thinking."

Kackle was so frustrated with Rudy. Kackle said, "Rudy, you're a crow. Remember our nestling days, our sharing bug sandwiches, playing start a rumor, and . . . and dive bombing all those clean windshields. We're brothers!"

Kackle put on his best pouting face. (This is not easy for a crow, since they have no lips.)

But Rudy knew what he had to do. Trembling, he took a deep breath.

"I need to find out who I am, Kackle," he said.

So, with all the courage that the young Rudy could muster, he left the crow flock in search of the truth.

Discussion Questions

1. The crows wanted Rudy to be a crow, but inside Rudy wanted to be an eagle. Kackle wanted Rudy to caw like a crow, but Rudy felt like screeching like an eagle. Describe a time when others wanted you to be someone you didn't want to be. Did you feel awkward? Why?

2. Why did Rudy leave the crows? Did Rudy make the right choice leaving the crows? Why?

3. Some friends may not give you the right information because they really don't know. They think they know, but they don't understand what is right for you. That is why we need mentors and a positive influence to help guide us with the right information. Why was Kackle and Hacker not a good influence for Rudy? They were his friends because they took care of him, but did they know how to help Rudy live his Dream? What would happen if Rudy listened to the crows?

RUDY'S 12 LESSONS FOR YOUNG CHAMPIONS

1. Develop your Dream and set realistic goals.

2. Get advice and good information from mentors who believe in your Dream.

3. Listen to good positive music, read positive books, and watch positive movies.

4. Hang out with friends that encourage you, not friends that put you down.

5. Always be a good example for others.

6. Inspire others to be their best.

7. Believe in yourself and take action. Action eliminates fear.

8. Prepare for your Dream, focus, and achieve your goals step by step.

9. Use anger in a positive way, to help you overcome your struggles and do something good.

10. Develop courage, faith, and wisdom and go for your Dream.

11. Have a "YES I CAN" attitude.

12. Never Quit!

- Chapter 9 -
Rudy and Bones

Night was falling when Rudy finally stopped to rest. Darkness filled the forest with strange, eerie night sounds. He heard sounds he had never noticed before.

Rudy's imagination began to play tricks on him. Tree branches became large monstrous claws, and every sound caused him to jump.

He was used to the comforting, yet sometimes aggravating sound of Kackle's snoring. He was scared, tired, and hungry. Yet he was also determined to spend the night away from the crows.

Rudy tried to find a comfortable perch in a small pine tree. Shivering, he ruffled his feathers and tucked his head to shield his face from the wind.

"Wwwwisskkk!" the wind whistled around him.

"Hey, kid, ppsssttt!" heard Rudy.

Rudy shuttered. Now he was hearing things.

"Hey, KID!" the voice yelled.

Rudy jumped. He thought, "That was definitely not the wind."

"Who, who, who's there?" Rudy asked nervously, while trying to sound fierce.

No answer. Silence. The only sound was the wind and those awful branches sounding like bones clanking together.

Rudy settled himself down once again and thought, "Funny how my imagination can play tricks on me."

Then he heard the voice again.

"Kid, over here." The voice was now sounding like a growl.

"Who said that? Better come out . . . or . . . crows will attack!" Rudy's voice quaked with fear.

All Rudy could hear was a faint hissing sound and the clanking of those branches.

The darkness closed in around him as the sound came closer. Though chilled from the night air, Rudy broke into a nervous sweat.

Rudy threw out another threat. "RRReally, really, crows will attack!" he warned and sounded even more scared.

He heard the voice again.

"Crows, indeed. I pick my teeth with crows," hissed the voice only inches from young Rudy's face.

In the darkness, Rudy could not make out the shape of the creature in front of him. Then, suddenly, the moon passed from behind the clouds.

All Rudy could see were two eyes. These eyes were huge, dark, and evil. These eyes had no sparkle of life. They had never known laughter. These eyes were unable to find beauty in a sunrise. These eyes were much too close for Rudy to feel safe. Rudy was frozen with fear as the stranger circled the small pine tree.

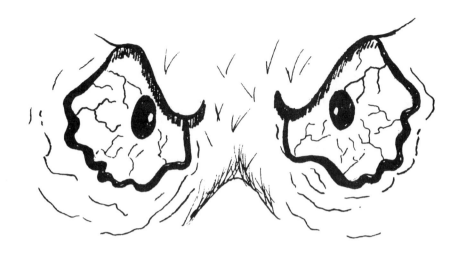

It was BONES, the vulture. Oh, how this vulture loved the smell of fear and the sweetness of stale sweat.

Bones paused and looked straight into Rudy's eyes. "Scared, aren't we?" he growled. He could sense Rudy's fear and smell Rudy's sweat. This made Bones feel so powerful.

Rudy just nodded that he was. He wanted to be brave and to stand up to this loathsome creature, but he was scared.

"Oh, pleasure, pleasure," Bones thought. He laughed as he drew closer to Rudy.

"Look deeply into my eyes," Bones ordered.

Rudy wanted to look away, or simply shut his eyes, but he couldn't. It was as if Rudy was in a trance. Then Bones put on a pair of dark glasses. The lenses looked like mirrors. They were distorted, awful mirrors.

"You think that Bones is scary?" he laughed. "Take a look at yourself. See how small, weak, and scared you are. Can you see all your failures?"

Bones could now see that Rudy was beginning to crumble. "That's it. Go ahead. It's easy. That's right. It's okay for you to lose all of your self-confidence, your ambitions, and your Dreams."

Rudy could see himself in the strange mirror becoming smaller and smaller. His desire to find out who he was became less important as he stared into Bones' glasses.

When only a tiny ember of hope remained in Rudy's reflection, Bones pulled himself away from looking at Rudy and started to sing and dance in the moonlight.

Just a little fear
pulls the attitude down.
A little fear,
and I'll start circling 'round;
fear of failure,
fear of success,
fear in itself, and
 your Dreams get left . . .
Yummy, yummy.
Oh yummy, yummy,
fear melts in Bones' tummy . . .

"Ah. You'll taste sweet, my young crowling," he said pausing as if to sniff the wind.

"Bones smells the sweetness of your fear. Yes. Bones can smell your ripe, sweet fear. But, crow? Bones does not sniff a crow . . . bird, to be sure. You are a scared bird, but not a crow. What kind of delicious, ripe, scared, and all-alone bird are we?" Bones probed as he drew closer and closer.

Rudy was certain that his end was near.

Bones took one last step toward Rudy. Suddenly, Bones' loathsome mouth formed into a soundless scream. Then . . . "AAAAAHHHHHHH!"

Bones began hopping on one foot.

"My precious, pink tootsie. Oh . . . oh . . . ouchy . . . oh!" he continued to yell.

Bones tumbled to the ground. His coat flew open and revealed hundreds and hundreds of skeleton bones of all shapes and sizes.

"Oh . . . tootsie . . . tootsie . . . tootsie!" Bones continued to wail as he held his scaly, shabby foot.

"Move! You are messing up my bristles, you smelly, cranky bone picker!" a muffled voice directly below Rudy cried.

Rudy leaned out of his perch. In the moonlight, he could see that beneath him was a porcupine.

The small, quilled creature was surrounded by a wide array of grooming tools and fancy-smelling goods.

Bones was in agony. He continued ranting. "Oh, the pain. Your awful bristles!

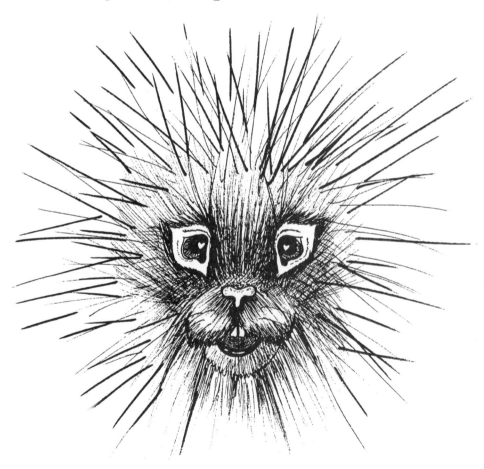

Horrible. Horrible. Your bristles are hooked to my pretty, pink tootsie. Take them out!" Bones stuck out his ugly foot.

"Pretty, pink tootsie, indeed," laughed the spunky little porcupine. "That is the ugliest foot I have ever seen."

"Please. Please. Please!" Bones pleaded.

The porcupine looked up at Rudy and winked. He smiled and said, "Sorry, Bones. I don't have the tools. It looks like you're hooked. You need to be more careful in the future. You were so focused on being nasty, mean, and unkind that you got yourself hooked by my bristles. Don't worry. After a couple of weeks and a little infection, you will hurt only when you think of me and the unfeeling way you were treating this poor little bird."

Before vanishing into the darkness, Bones quit hopping long enough to give Rudy one last menacing look.

Discussion Questions

1. How did Rudy feel his first night away from the crow flock?

2. How does Rudy see himself when he is with Bones? Why? How does Rudy see himself when he is with Yupper? Why? Describe the difference.

3. Why does Bones come after Rudy? How does Bones try to steal Rudy's Dream?

4. Who should Rudy listen to and spend time with? Why?

RUDY'S 12 LESSONS FOR YOUNG CHAMPIONS

1. Develop your Dream and set realistic goals.

2. Get advice and good information from mentors who believe in your Dream.

3. Listen to good positive music, read positive books, and watch positive movies.

4. Hang out with friends that encourage you, not friends that put you down.

5. Always be a good example for others.

6. Inspire others to be their best.

7. Believe in yourself and take action. Action eliminates fear.

8. Prepare for your Dream, focus, and achieve your goals step by step.

9. Use anger in a positive way, to help you overcome your struggles and do something good.

10. Develop courage, faith, and wisdom and go for your Dream.

11. Have a "YES I CAN" attitude.

12. Never Quit!

"Gee whiz. Thank you," Rudy said most appreciatively, as he climbed down from his perch. "I'm Rudy."

"Hello, Rudy . . . and you are very welcome. I'm Needles," said the young porcupine.

"Who was that?" asked Rudy.

"Congratulations. You just met Bones. He can be a pretty dangerous fellow, if you don't know how to deal with him," said Needles.

"I've never been so frightened!" Rudy exclaimed.

"That's the point," Needles continued. "Bones smells your fear and lack of confidence. He feeds on all of the negative thoughts and feelings you have about yourself."

"He was so ugly and scary. Then my reflection . . . it was not anything like I wanted it to be," said Rudy. "It's like this Needles . . . the crows put me down and Mr. Groundhog builds me up . . . I feel something inside, but I'm confused. I know I have a Dream! You see, my grandeagle was a Wind Dancer . . ."

"You were looking at yourself through Bones' eyes," interrupted the porcupine. "He wants you to see nothing. He wants you to feel like nothing and be nothing. He is not a friend."

Needles paused and smiled at Rudy, "I would like to be your friend."

The porcupine fluffed his quills and primped in his tiny mirror.

"Look at yourself through the eyes of a friend," offered Needles.

"I'm scared that I won't like what I see," Rudy cried.

"Think of your Dream. Imagine that you've already achieved it. Now look!" Needles instructed.

Rudy shut his eyes and tried to imagine himself as a Wind Dancer soaring high above the tree line. Then he opened his eyes and gazed at his reflection. What he saw amazed him.

He wasn't at all like the reflection he had seen in Bones' glasses. He was an eagle:

Strong, fearless, and wise. His eyes shined with an inner light. The only thing that seemed out of place was his crow colors. He reached up and touched his headband.

"Why do you wear crow colors?" Needles asked.

"I've been a part of the flock for such a long time. They accepted me," said Rudy.

"Did they see you as a crow or as an eagle?" asked Needles.

"I suppose as a crow," answered Rudy.

Once again he gazed into Needles' mirror. This time his reflection was that of a big, awkward crow. He now could see all of the weaknesses he had allowed himself to accept. He now realized that *fitting in* had become too high a price for him to pay and had cost him a great deal.

Needles looked at Rudy. "Rudy," he said, "do you think that I fit in? Do you know how many forest animals have told me that if I cut my quills, they would hug me? I would love to be hugged, but I'm going to be hugged for me. That's right, Rudy, quills

and all. I like who I am. I will find someone
to accept me, love me, and hug me just as I
am. You will see. Now Rudy, it seems to
me that you have much to think about."

After spending a restless night perched
in his small pine tree, Rudy opened his eyes.
Beside him was a note from Needles that
read,

Rudy,

Don't let anyone steal your Dream.
Others do not know what seeds of greatness are
within you. You have to believe in yourself
and Never Quit... only then can you make
your Dream come true
    You will not find the path to your Dream
in another's opinion of you. You must look
at yourself through your own eyes and follow
your heart.
    I have gone in search of my Dream.
Somewhere, someone will love me,
quills and all.

Your Friend,
Needles

Discussion Questions

1. Bones represents fear. Fear will try to stop you from your Dreams. What are some ways to overcome fear?

2. How do you see yourself when you are with a friend who believes in you?

3. What type of people do you need to be around to believe in yourself and develop self confidence?

4. What did Rudy see in Needles' mirror? Why was it different from what Rudy saw in Bones' glasses?

5. Imagine yourself living your Dream. What do you see? Draw a picture or write a story about your Dream.

6. Needles refused to cut his quills. Why?

7. Needles helped Rudy realize that "fitting in" with the crows had cost him a great deal. What did Rudy give up in order to "fit in"? What did Needles teach Rudy?

RUDY'S 12 LESSONS FOR YOUNG CHAMPIONS

1. Develop your Dream and set realistic goals.

2. Get advice and good information from mentors who believe in your Dream.

3. Listen to good positive music, read positive books, and watch positive movies.

4. Hang out with friends that encourage you, not friends that put you down.

5. Always be a good example for others.

6. Inspire others to be their best.

7. Believe in yourself and take action. Action eliminates fear.

8. Prepare for your Dream, focus, and achieve your goals step by step.

9. Use anger in a positive way, to help you overcome your struggles and do something good.

10. Develop courage, faith, and wisdom and go for your Dream.

11. Have a "YES I CAN" attitude.

12. Never Quit!

- Chapter 11 -
Rudy and Bellows

The morning fog lay low over the meadows. When Rudy looked down on the thick
mist, he began to visualize his Dream.
"This is how eagles see clouds," he thought.

The sight was beautiful as the sun filtered
through the mist below him. For a moment, young Rudy pretended he was an
eagle, even a Wind Dancer.

Lost in his fantasy, he hopped out of his tree. The fog was so thick that he couldn't see one foot in front of him. He was not sure of which way to go. He stretched his neck and peeked above the fog. He could see that the forest was in the distance now, and it seemed that he was in the center of the meadow.

Suddenly, the earth beneath him shook. It sounded like thunder. Frightened, Rudy stood and watched. At first, there appeared to be leafless tree limbs rising out of the mist. Then the sun's intense rays burned away enough mist and he could see that these were not tree limbs. Instead, they were antlers. He now found himself sur-rounded by huge, magnificent bull elks.

What Rudy didn't know was that this was the first day of *The Rutting Season*. All the bull elks had gathered at Daisy Meadows for the annual Buck Tournament.

The buck next to Rudy raised his mighty head and let out a huge bellow, "AAAAAHHHHHRRROOOOO!"

Terrified, Rudy froze as the elks began to charge. Just when it seemed that he was sure to be crushed, something or someone tossed him into the air.

"Hey Bird, you had better fly or you'll get stomped on," said the elk.

"What is happening?" asked Rudy.

"Here," the buck nosed Rudy up onto a stump, "sit up here where it's safe and cheer for me. I'm Bellows!"

As the elk trotted back to the tournament, he limped slightly. It was then that Rudy noticed that Bellows wore a brace on his hind leg.

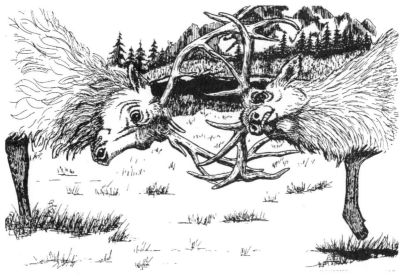

Rudy watched in amazement as the elks bucked and tumbled one another across the meadow. The air was charged with excitement. Antlers were hitting antlers. The thundering sound of hooves filled the air. The contest of strength continued until only the two strongest bulls faced off.

It was Bellows against an older, larger, more seasoned bull. The older bull strutted around his end of the field. He had won many Buck Tournaments, and he was confident that today would be no different.

But Bellows was focused. This was the day that he had prepared for all season. It would be his only chance to claim territory until next year.

Rudy trembled as he watched them lower their mighty heads, paw the ground, and charge.

CRASH! Their antlers collided.

"Go, Bellows. Push to the left of him. Now, over to the right. Go, Go, Go, Bellows!" Rudy yelled.

The two bulls struggled back and forth.

"You can do it, Bellows!" Rudy assured as he cheered for his new friend.

First, the older bull would gain ground, then Bellows would struggle and regain the ground he had lost. The battle went on, endlessly, until steam and sweat rolled off both of them.

Finally, the older bull lowered his head several inches and gave a mighty push. Bellows' hind feet almost touched the outer boundary limits of the Meadow. If either of their feet touched outside the Meadow's field, they would be disqualified. For a few seconds, it seemed that Bellows might lose.

Then Bellows lowered his head, took a deep breath and let out a loud "AAHHHHRROOO!" With all his might, he pushed the older bull clear across the boundary.

A cheer arose from the elks. The two bulls bowed respectfully to one another.

Rudy watched with pride as his new friend received *The Medallion of Courage.*

Then, Rudy hopped over to Bellows and said, "Wow! You were great."

"Thanks," smiled Bellows.

"I'm Rudy," Rudy said.

"Well, Rudy bird, it is nice to meet you. When the elks were charging, I thought you were a goner. You could have been stomped to death. Why didn't you fly to safety?" Bellows inquired.

"Gosh, there wasn't any tree to fly to . . . and, and, and, it all happened so fast," Rudy tried to explain and excuse his behavior.

"A big bird like you doesn't need trees. Why, if I had your wings, I would head for the clouds," said Bellows looking at the sky above him.

"I've never flown above the tree line," Rudy said a little embarrassed. "We crows can only fly so high, you know."

"CROWS?" Bellows laughed. "Is that why you are wearing crow colors? You think you're a crow? I'm no expert, but it seems to me that you're a bit more than a common crow."

"Ever since I joined the crows, I've been told that I was a crow," Rudy said. "Besides, I have a bum wing."

"What's wrong with it?" asked Bellows.

"I fell on it, and since then I haven't been able to stretch it out. I tried a couple of times, but it hurt," Rudy explained.

Bellows looked at Rudy. "Rudy, when I was a tiny fawn, I broke my hind leg. At first they said I'd never walk, run, or jump. But, my grandelk told me to keep trying. It hurt, but little by little, I got stronger."

With that, Bellows jumped around on his braced leg to show Rudy how much he had improved.

"Gosh, Bellows, do you think that I could overcome having a bad wing?" Rudy asked.

"I just know that I'd never quit trying. Why are you hanging out with the crows, anyway?" Bellows asked.

"I guess that it has been easier to be one of them. I didn't have to even think for myself. They really took care of me. They told me how to dress, what to eat, and how to fly. But, now I don't know what I want. I really need to find out who I am," answered Rudy.

"What kind of bird do you want to be?" Bellows asked.

"Promise not to laugh?" Rudy asked shyly.

"I promise," said Bellows.

"An eagle. Even more than an eagle. I want to be a Wind Dancer," whispered Rudy.

"Man. You sure know how to Dream big," laughed Bellows.

"You're laughing," said Rudy.

"No, no, my friend. I am not laughing at your Dream. I am just surprised at how big your Dream is. You see, Rudy, I have a big Dream too. If you can have the courage to be an eagle, then I can have the heart to jump Monarch Canyon," explained Bellows.

Rudy followed Bellows down a well-worn path that led to the edge of a long, narrow valley between two high cliffs. Rudy was breathless as he looked over the edge. It was ever-so-far to the bottom.

"Goodness, Bellows, aren't you afraid of falling?" asked Rudy.

"A little bit," confessed Bellows, "but I am even more afraid of never trying and letting go of my Dream."

Bellows snorted and pawed the ground.

"Someday, I'm going to just go for it," Bellows shouted joyfully. "I'll jump over this canyon, Rudy, and have the freedom to feed in any pasture I want. Just like someday I'll look up there above the clouds and I'll see, you, a Wind Dancer. You will be magnificent, soaring and gliding in those mountain currents. Remember, never forget your Dream, Rudy. Only you can make it happen."

"The crows always told me that I could never be anything but a crow," Rudy explained. "When you talk, I feel that it would not only be possible, but easy to become a Wind Dancer."

Bellows lowered his head and looked into Rudy's eyes. "Rudy," said Bellows, "when you believe in yourself and your Dream, you can do anything! But it is never easy to

achieve your Dream. It takes courage. It will require much work. I know that I'll never fly because I don't have wings, but I have powerful legs. I can jump over Monarch Canyon."

"Rudy, you're not a crow. You're an eagle. The crows don't have enough faith to rise above the tree line," he added.

"Believe in yourself, Rudy! Have faith! You will be a Wind Dancer!" cheered Bellows.

Bellows took the medallion he'd won in the Buck Tournament and slipped it over Rudy's head. "Here," he said, "keep this as a symbol of what we are yet to achieve."

Rudy's eyes filled with tears. "You are the best friend I ever had!" he whispered.

Discussion Questions

1. In the morning mist, Rudy began to visualize his Dream. Why is it important to visualize your Dream?

2. What did Bellows and Rudy have in common?

3. How does Rudy feel when he is with Bellows?

4. How did Bellows inspire Rudy?

5. Both Rudy and Bellows have physical challenges to overcome. Why is there still hope for them to achieve their Dreams? What must they do? Are living Dreams easy? Why?

6. Is Bellows a mentor for Rudy? Why?

RUDY'S 12 LESSONS FOR YOUNG CHAMPIONS

1. Develop your Dream and set realistic goals.

2. Get advice and good information from mentors who believe in your Dream.

3. Listen to good positive music, read positive books, and watch positive movies.

4. Hang out with friends that encourage you, not friends that put you down.

5. Always be a good example for others.

6. Inspire others to be their best.

7. Believe in yourself and take action. Action eliminates fear.

8. Prepare for your Dream, focus, and achieve your goals step by step.

9. Use anger in a positive way, to help you overcome your struggles and do something good.

10. Develop courage, faith, and wisdom and go for your Dream.

11. Have a "YES I CAN" attitude.

12. Never Quit!

- Chapter 12 -
Bellows and Courage

From the far north thunder rumbled. Rudy and Bellows looked anxiously at the sky. They could see the blackest of clouds gathering in the distance. All around them came a sharp whistling of the wind.

"Looks like a nasty storm is heading this way," said Bellows. "We had better warn the other animals. I'll go look after the elk herd, Rudy, and you gather the others at the high meadow. They will be safer there."

"Be careful!" Rudy cautioned as Bellows ran as fast as the wind through the field.

Rudy began to alert all the animals. "Quick, run for the high meadow," Rudy screamed to the animals as he began to fly and run, fly and run.

He banged on Yupper's door with his outstretched wing. "Yupper!" he yelled. "A storm is coming. Come on, open your door. Yupper, run! A storm is coming. You must run to the high meadow."

Yupper opened his door.

"Dag nabit, Rudy. What are you screaming about?" he asked.

He didn't need Rudy to answer. One glance told him that danger was close at hand.

"Oh my, I suppose I'll be cleaning up after this one for a month. YUP, YUP . . . I better run!" he shouted.

Yupper hurried down the path. He called to Rudy, "You get to safety, and I'll get the others. That's an order. You hear?"

By the time Rudy and the others made their way to the high meadow, it was getting very dark. The wind was howling horribly. Forest animals and birds were still hurrying along to reach the high meadow. Tree branches were crashing down around them, and every few minutes lightening lit up the sky as brightly as the sun.

"Where is Bellows?" Rudy wondered. He began to make his way through the crowd to look for Bellows. It was difficult to see. There were so many frightened animals and birds all around.

Finally, a flash of lightening lit up the meadow and Rudy saw Bellows. He was trying to comfort and calm the does and fawns. Rudy flew above the crowd to reach Bellows. For a moment the storm grew still.

A loud "SCHREECCHH" pierced the air. Rudy looked up into the sky and saw a magnificent eagle trying to land. Rudy tried to dodge out of the eagle's way, for they were sure to crash into one another. The great eagle folded its wings and in spite of the strong winds, it landed skillfully in front of Rudy. As he stared into the eagle's beautiful, deep golden eyes, he began to remember . . .

"Mother?" he asked.

"Rudy? Is that you, my son?" she asked nervously. It had been so long, she could hardly believe that he had survived! But, she knew that, somehow, he was different.

"Where have you been Rudy? I thought you were lost forever . . . and why are you wearing crow colors? Are you all right, Rudy?" she questioned.

Before Rudy could answer, the cry of a lost, frightened fawn came from the edge of the forest. The poor, tiny creature was huddled, crying beneath a huge elm tree.

What happened next happened very quickly.

Thunder rumbled as Bellows charged across the meadow to rescue the fawn. Once again, lightening lit up the sky. A

blinding white flash hit the top of the elm tree. The fawn lay paralyzed with fear as the tree began to fall. The distance between Bellows and the panic-stricken fawn was twice that of Monarch Canyon. It looked to be an impossible leap.

Bellows gathered his strength and with a mighty "AAAAAHHHHRROOOOOO," leaped. Rudy and the animals held their breath as Bellows landed squarely in front of the frightened fawn. With no time to spare, Bellows pushed the fawn to safety.

"Bellows!" Rudy screamed as the tree exploded with fire.

For a brief moment, Rudy thought Bellows would be quick enough to jump out of its path, but Bellows couldn't judge which way to jump. Rudy and the other animals watched in horror as the tree came crashing down, pinning and crushing Bellows beneath it.

Rudy was screaming, "Bellows, Bellows!

No, No!" Leaving his mother and the other animals, he flew to the burning tree. Rudy's mother wondered if she would ever see him again.

Bellows was gasping for air as Rudy tried to lift the tree from his body. Fire nipped at Rudy's wings and feet as he desperately struggled with the impossible weight.

"Rudy," Bellows gasped.

147

Rudy bent down beside his friend. "Rudy, I could have cleared Monarch Canyon," said Bellows struggling to speak.

"Bellows, you could have cleared two Monarch Canyons," Rudy sobbed.

Bellows took his last breath and said, "Rudy, never let your Dream die. Remember, NEVER, NEVER QUIT!"

Through a flood of tears Rudy said, "Bellows, the Dream will never die, my friend." Rudy promised and then tore away his crow colors.

Suddenly, the rains came.

Wet and chilled to the bone, young Rudy sat beside his friend and cried until the tears would come no more.

Discussion Questions

1. What was Bellows' act of courage?

2. What lesson did Rudy learn from Bellows' death?

3. What did Rudy do as a symbol that he was ready to pursue his Dream?

4. When Rudy met his mother again it triggered his memory. What do you think Rudy began to remember?

5. What obstacles did Bellows have to overcome to make his jump? Why was his jump important?

RUDY'S 12 LESSONS FOR YOUNG CHAMPIONS

1. Develop your Dream and set realistic goals.

2. Get advice and good information from mentors who believe in your Dream.

3. Listen to good positive music, read positive books, and watch positive movies.

4. Hang out with friends that encourage you, not friends that put you down.

5. Always be a good example for others.

6. Inspire others to be their best.

7. Believe in yourself and take action. Action eliminates fear.

8. Prepare for your Dream, focus, and achieve your goals step by step.

9. Use anger in a positive way, to help you overcome your struggles and do something good.

10. Develop courage, faith, and wisdom and go for your Dream.

11. Have a "YES I CAN" attitude.

12. Never Quit!

- *Chapter 13* -
Rudy Pursues the Dream

The next day, Rudy found his way to the river. He felt an emptiness deep inside.

Bellows had lifted his hopes and Dreams so high. The thought of that friendship being gone forever caused Rudy such pain. It was so great a burden to bear. He sat with his eyes shut and listened to the wind whistling through the tree tops.

"Does the wind call to you, little one?" said a voice. Rudy jumped. He had thought he was alone.

Perched on a boulder beside Rudy was a magnificent Golden Eagle. His bronze and golden feathers glistened in the sun like rare jewels. His eyes were amazing. Rudy shivered. He felt like the eagle could see right through him.

"Yes, it does," Rudy said.

"It's such a lovely sound to hear the wind dancing with the trees," said the magnificent eagle. He shut his piercing eyes and

155

let the sound wash over him. "It's much like Wind Dancing," said the Golden Eagle.

"Are you a Wind Dancer?" asked Rudy.

"The question is, young eagle, are you a Wind Dancer?" asked the Golden Eagle.

"I don't know," responded Rudy. "I now know that I am not a crow. Bellows, my best friend, is gone. He made me feel like

an eagle. I could Dream of becoming a Wind Dancer, like my grandeagle. He had faith in me and my Dream." Rudy's eyes filled with pain.

The Golden Eagle spoke. "Perhaps he is still with you. Is it possible that his true purpose in life was not to complete his Dream, but to inspire you to believe in yourself and achieve your Dream? Did he not truly touch your heart and inspire you?"

"Yes, he did," answered Rudy. "Bellows leaped further than he ever Dreamed he could, and he taught me to never quit."

"Then he is not gone," the Golden Eagle replied. "His lessons will remain with you forever."

Rudy gently touched his medallion. "Before I met Bellows, I thought I was a crow. I didn't believe that I could be a Wind Dancer."

The Golden Eagle threw back his head and laughed. "Ah, yes, the crows . . . interesting group. They certainly know how to make noise, but they rarely say anything truthful. They flutter and flap and call it flying, but they go nowhere."

"But, how could I ever fly so high? The currents are so strong. I need to learn what to do. I'm afraid that I would be thrown to the ground. I tried to fly a long time ago and injured my wing," Rudy remembered. "Besides, my feathers are not as powerful as yours. I don't know how to read the winds."

"When Bellows asked you what you wanted to be, you said an eagle, a Wind Dancer. Didn't you?" asked the Golden Eagle.

"Yes," Rudy answered.

"Why do you want to be a Wind Dancer, Rudy?" the Golden Eagle asked.

Before he answered, Rudy thought, ". . . it would be incredible to own the sky, to soar, and to dance with the wind. I would love to be able to fly to any mountaintop. If I were a Wind Dancer, I could fly through the storms. I could tame the violent winds and make them appear as calm as a summer's day . . . that would be great. But more importantly, I love all the animals of the forest. The different kinds of birds and all the funny and fuzzy creatures are my friends. If the animals could see what I have achieved, then they would be encouraged to overcome their struggles and achieve their Dreams . . ."

"To inspire others to be their best!" Rudy yelled, filled with emotion. "What must I do?"

The Golden Eagle smiled warmly and proudly at Rudy's insight, sensitivity, and desire to share.

The Golden Eagle advised, "Begin now to prepare. Listen to the trees. Study the clouds and learn the wind. Continue to grow wiser as your body continues to grow stronger and stronger. If you never quit, the time will come when you will have courage, faith, wisdom, and the knowledge to make your Dreams come true."

With great strength and confidence the Golden Eagle continued, "It is preparation that gives you the knowledge and wisdom. You will learn from your struggles, Rudy. But, it is faith that gives you the courage to prepare. First you must believe, Rudy.

Then, take action. Step by step you will learn, and step by step you will achieve your Dream."

The mighty Golden Eagle spread his powerful wings and cried out, "Rudy, Believe! Your grandeagle lives in you!" With a giant sweep of his wings, he flew into the rays of the sun.

Rudy blinked his eyes and the Golden Eagle was gone.

"Courage, faith, wisdom," Rudy whispered these words over and over to himself. These words played such an important part in his Dream.

He thought back to Bellows. Bellows had such courage, faith, and wisdom. He had been so wonderful. He had generously shared these qualities with all that he touched. Rudy was beginning to understand.

But faith was like the wind. It was not something that you could see or capture, but only feel. Rudy had to get in touch with his feelings. He now remembered back to the story of his grandeagle, the great Wind Dancer. His grandeagle possessed not only faith, but also wisdom and courage. A wave of hope and excitement now fired him up.

"I AM GOING TO BE A GREAT EAGLE. I AM GOING TO BE A WIND DANCER," he loudly proclaimed.

His voice echoed through the mountains and valleys, declaring his Dream to all.

Rudy knew that some of the crows would laugh. Some would even react with anger and disbelief. He wouldn't let their reaction hold him back.

Discussion Questions

1. Explain what Rudy learned from the Golden Eagle. Why is it important to prepare? How do you get knowledge and wisdom? Why is faith important?

2. Why does Rudy want to become a Wind Dancer? What other benefits would Rudy gain by achieving his Dream? How would Rudy affect others by living his Dream?

3. Think of your Dream. Why do you want to live your Dream?

4. List some of your struggles and describe what you learned from them.

5. Why is it important to never give up?

RUDY'S 12 LESSONS FOR YOUNG CHAMPIONS

1. Develop your Dream and set realistic goals.

2. Get advice and good information from mentors who believe in your Dream.

3. Listen to good positive music, read positive books, and watch positive movies.

4. Hang out with friends that encourage you, not friends that put you down.

5. Always be a good example for others.

6. Inspire others to be their best.

7. Believe in yourself and take action. Action eliminates fear.

8. Prepare for your Dream, focus, and achieve your goals step by step.

9. Use anger in a positive way, to help you overcome your struggles and do something good.

10. Develop courage, faith, and wisdom and go for your Dream.

11. Have a "YES I CAN" attitude.

12. Never Quit!

- Chapter 14 -
Rudy Prepares

The wind was high in the tree tops. Strong
gusts swept down over the river bank. It
felt cool and wonderful on Rudy's face.
Bravely, he climbed onto the top of a boulder and spread his wings, just as the Golden
Eagle had done.

The wind was even stronger now. He could feel it gathering strength beneath his feathers. He stretched his wings to almost their full length. His injured wing cramped, but he ignored the pain.

With one powerful sweep, he rose. Gathering speed and strength, he started to rise above the tree line. Then, suddenly, a gust of wind caught him unaware and Rudy began to tumble wildly out of control toward the ground.

Upside down and round and round he went until SPLASH, he landed in the river.

Battered, bruised, and gasping for breath, Rudy wondered what he had done wrong. He had used all the courage, faith, and wisdom he could muster, and still he had failed.

Then, he heard Bellows' voice in his head, "Rudy, never let your Dream die. Remember, NEVER, NEVER QUIT!"

Next Rudy remembered the words of the Golden Eagle, "PREPARE. Listen to the trees. Study the clouds and learn the wind . . . when you have learned from your struggles and the time is right, you will live your Dream . . ."

Rudy continued to think of the encouraging messages from his great friends.

Rudy now told himself, "I must never quit. I must never give up the Dream. I must prepare." Rudy wiped away his tears.

Courage, faith, and wisdom were not enough. Now Rudy must prepare and take action. He must get back up and try again. He must gather the knowledge necessary to achieve his Dream.

Discussion Questions

1. What helps Rudy to get back up and never quit?

2. What helps you to get through your struggles? a special person? a thought? a song? a movie? What encourages you to keep going?

3. We can't just sit back and wait for our Dreams to happen. We must work hard, struggle, and put forth much effort. Besides having Courage, Faith, and Wisdom, what else must Rudy do to become a Wind Dancer? Why was this advice from the Golden Eagle important?

RUDY'S 12 LESSONS FOR YOUNG CHAMPIONS

1. Develop your Dream and set realistic goals.

2. Get advice and good information from mentors who believe in your Dream.

3. Listen to good positive music, read positive books, and watch positive movies.

4. Hang out with friends that encourage you, not friends that put you down.

5. Always be a good example for others.

6. Inspire others to be their best.

7. Believe in yourself and take action. Action eliminates fear.

8. Prepare for your Dream, focus, and achieve your goals step by step.

9. Use anger in a positive way, to help you overcome your struggles and do something good.

10. Develop courage, faith, and wisdom and go for your Dream.

11. Have a "YES I CAN" attitude.

12. Never Quit!

- Chapter 15 -
Rudy Struggles

Rudy quickly discovered that Bellows had been right. Dreams do not come easy. Fitting in with the crows had come with the high price of letting go of his Dream. Now, achieving the Dream of becoming a Wind Dancer also comes with a high price. It would take much effort.

Rudy had to make wise choices. He had to decide how to spend his time. He was careful about with whom he spent his time. He tried to hang out with mentors that encouraged him and believed in his Dream. He made friends with the forest animals who had Dreams of their own, so they could inspire each other to be their best.

This was not always easy because he was forever running into the crow gang.

Kackle missed Rudy and desperately wanted him to come back to the crows. At times, Rudy was lonely. He still cared about his old friends. But, when they pestered him and told him to give up on that crazy eagle stuff, Rudy remembered his promise to Bellows. "Never, Never Quit!"

Rudy learned to tune out the words of the crows. His Dream was too important to let the crows hold him back. Rudy made the decision to avoid the crows. He had to focus.

Early every morning, even before the early birds left their nest, Rudy was up stretching and exercising his wings. It took time, but that once-injured wing began to get stronger and stronger. As it grew stronger, so did Rudy and his determination.

 He fed his still-growing body wholesome food and stayed clear of the garbage cans. This took time. It was more difficult to find nutritious food than it was to raid the trash, but Rudy wanted his body to be strong.

Time passed. Each and every day Rudy studied and trained and trained and studied. He practiced and practiced to understand the wind. He spent his time listening to the flow of the currents. He talked to many mentors and asked them to share their knowledge with him.

Rudy spoke of his Dream to all that would listen. Some offered words of encouragement, while others reacted with disbelief. Some even mocked him, but Rudy never wavered in his determination to fulfill his Dream and become a Wind Dancer.

Discussion Questions

1. How did Rudy prepare for his Dream?

2. What decisions did Rudy have to make to focus on his Dream? What did he decide when the crows told him to give up that crazy eagle stuff? Why was this a good decision?

3. What do you need to do to prepare for your Dream?

RUDY'S 12 LESSONS FOR YOUNG CHAMPIONS

1. Develop your Dream and set realistic goals.

2. Get advice and good information from mentors who believe in your Dream.

3. Listen to good positive music, read positive books, and watch positive movies.

4. Hang out with friends that encourage you, not friends that put you down.

5. Always be a good example for others.

6. Inspire others to be their best.

7. Believe in yourself and take action. Action eliminates fear.

8. Prepare for your Dream, focus, and achieve your goals step by step.

9. Use anger in a positive way, to help you overcome your struggles and do something good.

10. Develop courage, faith, and wisdom and go for your Dream.

11. Have a "YES I CAN" attitude.

12. Never Quit!

- Chapter 16 -
Rudy Learns from the Wind

Then there was Hacker. Hacker was his old crow nestmate. He taunted Rudy.

"Well, what's stopping you?" Hacker challenged. "Go ahead and do it. Are you an eagle or a chicken?" Hacker and the other crows jeered.

Rudy's eyes were filled with determination. He was angry. But it was not the kind of anger that is destructive and makes you less than you are, but the kind of anger that makes you more determined.

Rudy threw back his head and SCHREECHED! He spread his wings to their full length. They were awesome. His wings were larger now than anyone had ever seen. The once-injured wing was now strong and steady.

With one powerful downward stroke, he rose. SWOOSH! The power of his take off silenced the mocking crows. Soon the tree line and the crows were far below.

"I AM AN EAGLE!" he screamed.

The wind shifted. Rudy adjusted his wings and caught the current just right. He effortlessly continued to rise.

"YUP, YUP . . . now, there goes an eagle," Yupper proudly proclaimed.

"Yeah, an eagle for sure," agreed Kackle.

The other crows continued to grumble in amazement.

Rudy circled with the wind and approached Monarch Canyon. Suddenly, an upward draft from the canyon pushed him into a crosswind. This caught him from

behind and propelled him toward the canyon. Rudy desperately tried to adjust, but the current was too strong. Rudy began to lose control.

The fall seemed endless. Over and over he tumbled, past the tree line, past Yupper and the crows, and down into the canyon's deepest depths.

"Rudy!" cried Yupper and Kackle. They feared for their friend's life. They hurried down the side of the canyon.

"No one, not even an eagle, could survive that fall," mumbled the crow flock.

Discussion Questions

1. Rudy uses anger in a positive way. It gives him energy and helps him to be more determined. We do not want to use anger to destroy or do something bad. We want to use it to help us to overcome our struggles and do something good. In what ways does anger help Rudy?

2. Describe a time when you were angry. What did you do? After learning from Rudy, what would you do differently?

3. Describe how Rudy continues to struggle.

RUDY'S 12 LESSONS FOR YOUNG CHAMPIONS

1. Develop your Dream and set realistic goals.

2. Get advice and good information from mentors who believe in your Dream.

3. Listen to good positive music, read positive books, and watch positive movies.

4. Hang out with friends that encourage you, not friends that put you down.

5. Always be a good example for others.

6. Inspire others to be their best.

7. Believe in yourself and take action. Action eliminates fear.

8. Prepare for your Dream, focus, and achieve your goals step by step.

9. Use anger in a positive way, to help you overcome your struggles and do something good.

10. Develop courage, faith, and wisdom and go for your Dream.

11. Have a "YES I CAN" attitude.

12. Never Quit!

- *Chapter 17* -
Rudy Meets the Challenge

Far below, young Rudy lay bruised and bleeding. As he caught his breath, his eyes filled with tears. Fear and doubt began to seep into his heart.

"I can't do this anymore," he whispered to himself.

Just then, a shadow passed over him from above, a dark and sinister shadow. Then, Rudy heard the voice that he'd hoped he'd never hear again.

"Ah sweets.

Blood and fear . . .

It draws Bones near."

Bones sang as he hovered above the
canyon's currents.

"The current's strong, but sweet is fear . . .

I'll circle 'round and land down here.

Bones will come to you, my sweets . . .

Soon.

Very soon."

Bones left to enter the canyon in a place where the wind was less dangerous.

Rudy shut his eyes and began to tremble.

"I have prepared and worked so hard. I believe. I have courage. I have faith. I have wisdom. Yet, I still failed. How will I ever succeed at becoming a Wind Dancer?" Rudy said with determination.

A hand touched Rudy's shoulder. It was Yupper.

"You can't fail if you never quit," Yupper said, and Kackle nodded.

"Yupper? Kackle?" Rudy was relieved to see his two friends.

"Why . . . you're already a success, young Rudy, 'cause you ain't never quit. Right, Kackle?" Yupper elbowed Kackle.

"Yeah, yeah Rudy. You're no crow, you know," Kackle added.

Yupper said, "RUDY, DON'T BECOME A WIND DANCER TO PROVE SOMETHING TO THE CROWS, OR TO ME. BECOME A WIND DANCER FOR YOURSELF. YOUR DREAM MUST BE INSIDE YOU, RUDY. GIVE YOURSELF SOMETHING TO CHEER FOR. BELIEVE IN YOURSELF AND BECOME THE WIND DANCER THAT IS LOCKED WITHIN YOU."

Just then, Bones' shadow entered the canyon and warned them of his approach.

"Bones is coming for me. What'll I do?" Rudy cried.

"LEAVE HIM ALONE!" Yupper yelled as he attacked Bones with his broom.

"Yeah . . . let him be!" Kackle chimed in.

"Nasty ole bone collector. You ain't adding a young eagle bird to that smelly cape you're wearing!" Yupper assured as he waved his broom at Bones like a warrior's sword.

"My sweets, an eagle?" Bones laughed.

198

"An eagle indeed.

This bird has less guts

than a little mustard seed.

I'll pick his bones.

It'll be child's-play.

An eagle indeed.

There ain't no way,

ain't no way . . .

Just ain't no way."

"Now, be gone before Bones acquires a taste for tough ole groundhogs and scrawny crows. It's his fear that draws Bones near," Bones said as he bullied his way past Yupper and Kackle.

Yupper reminded Rudy, "He comes to feed on your fear, Rudy. No one else can save you because the fear's inside you. I can't

save you from yourself. But you can fight him, Rudy. Show him no fear."

"You have the courage, faith, and wisdom to make it happen. What'll you say when those *canters* tell you that Rudy CAN'T. Never be a *canter*. You're a Wind Dancer! Remember what old Yupper told you about *canters*," he added.

Rudy shut his eyes tight. Behind him he could hear the sound of Bones clanking. He knew the vulture was approaching.

Rudy whispered to himself, "Yes I Can."

He tried to remember all of those things that had encouraged and inspired him to Dream. He could now hear the words of his Mother, Yupper, Needles, Bellows, and the Golden Eagle. He could feel their encouragement and strength building inside him. "YES I CAN! YES I CAN! YES I CAN!" Rudy thought.

Rudy's spirit began to soar.

He looked above at the impossible leap that had been his friend's Dream.

"AAAHHHHRRRROOOOO," Bellows' voice rang clear in Rudy's head and heart.

"Never, never quit!" whispered the wind.

Courage, faith, and wisdom burst inside him. He now truly possessed the heart of a Wind Dancer. The time had come, and he was prepared. Rudy was no longer afraid.

"AIN'T NO WAY!" called the voice from behind him. Rudy could feel and smell Bones' rotten breath upon his neck, but it caused him no fear or dread.

Bones was quite sure of himself. He was confident that the bird in front of him was totally defenseless and ready to become another one of his victims. Bones began hopping from foot to foot in delicious anticipation.

"Turn around, my sweets. Let Bones see the fear in your eyes. Ha . . . an eagle, indeed . . . there ain't no way," snarled the buzzard.

Rudy began to rise and slowly turn. He lifted his head.

"YES I CAN!" Rudy screamed.

"AAAHHHH!" Bones screamed and shielded himself with his cape.

Before Bones stood a magnificent, fully-grown eagle. Rudy's wings were sleek and shined like polished copper. His regal head was now snow white. His eyes were pure gold. This brought the most terror to Bones.

Rudy's eyes shined with a wealth of knowledge, courage, faith, and wisdom. They went through Bones like a laser. Under Rudy's direct stare, Bones began to smoke and smolder.

"No fair!" Bones cried as he tripped and stumbled in his effort to retreat.

Discussion Questions

1. Why did Yupper tell Rudy he was already a success? Yupper also told Rudy to become a Wind Dancer for himself, not to prove something to someone else. Why is that advice important?

2. Kackle loved Rudy and always tried to defend him. How does Kackle show his loyalty to Rudy in chapter 17?
What does Kackle say to help Rudy?

3. What actions and thoughts help Rudy overcome fear?

4. Who has encouraged Rudy to live his Dream? Why is encouragement important for Rudy at this time in his life?

5. How does Rudy confront Bones? Why is Bones now afraid of Rudy?

6. What actions and thoughts help you overcome fear?

RUDY'S 12 LESSONS FOR YOUNG CHAMPIONS

1. Develop your Dream and set realistic goals.

2. Get advice and good information from mentors who believe in your Dream.

3. Listen to good positive music, read positive books, and watch positive movies.

4. Hang out with friends that encourage you, not friends that put you down.

5. Always be a good example for others.

6. Inspire others to be their best.

7. Believe in yourself and take action. Action eliminates fear.

8. Prepare for your Dream, focus, and achieve your goals step by step.

9. Use anger in a positive way, to help you overcome your struggles and do something good.

10. Develop courage, faith, and wisdom and go for your Dream.

11. Have a "YES I CAN" attitude.

12. Never Quit!

- Chapter 18 -
Rudy and the Battle

Within the canyon, the wind whirled violently around Rudy. Rising above the tremendously strong tornado like winds would be an impossible feat for any bird, other than a Wind Dancer.

The time had come for him to fulfill the Dream for which he had prepared. Once again, he spread his mighty wings.

This time there was no hesitation in his heart. There was only joy and the eagerness that comes with having faith from within. Rudy took a deep breath and shut his eyes.

"I have courage. I have faith. I have wisdom. I CAN WIND DANCE! YES I CAN. YES I CAN!" he cried. With a mighty downward stroke of his powerful wings, Rudy flew into the wind like a rocket.

The first current almost flung him into the side of the canyon wall. But with a graceful tilt of his wings, he caught a western wind, which almost allowed him to exit the canyon.

Then, suddenly, a down draft propelled him into a spin. Instead of frantically flapping his wings, he simply folded them and dove down. Just at the right moment, he once again spread his wings and caught an incredibly strong upward current.

Higher and higher he was able to soar. Higher and higher he went.

Rudy's spirit began to soar even more.

Only the force of the canyon's wind could break his focus. The currents were now stronger than ever. Rudy would have to match his skill to winds of near-hurricane force. Nature's worst!

Yupper and Kackle began to fear for Rudy's very life. They had never seen such a raging wind. Lightning crackled from above as Rudy struggled. The roar of the wind within the canyon walls was deafening.

"THE SECRETS OF THE MOUNTAIN CURRENTS ARE MINE. YOU CAN'T HAVE THEM!" screamed the wind.

"RUDY . . . WHAT DO YOU SAY TO
CANTERS?" Yupper hollered from below.

"YES I CAN!" Rudy screeched. He
turned and flew into the raging wind. He
was ready to face his greatest challenge.
The wind could not control a Wind Dancer.
A Wind Dancer controls the wind. The
storm howled and roared. It attempted to
grab Rudy and dash him into the cliffs.
But, he continued to dance, dodge, and
soar. Rudy took control and made the wind
appear to be as gentle as a summer's breeze.

Discussion Questions

1. How has Rudy changed? What elements does he now possess?

2. How did Rudy inspire all the other animals?

3. What were Rudy's obstacles throughout his journey?

4. Should you quit on your Dream when you hit obstacles? What would Bellows say to that?

5. How did Rudy overcome those obstacles?

6. Rudy learned lessons from his different mentors. What did he learn from:

Yupper?
Needles?
Bellows?
Golden Eagle?
His Mother?

7. Who are some of your mentors? a family member? a character in a story? a person in a movie? a hero? How do they help you?

8. List your struggles and obstacles. What must you do to overcome them? How must you think? What characteristics would you look for in a mentor?

9. Most people have Dreams, but do not always have the courage to pursue them. What steps must you take to achieve your Dream? What must you do to prepare?

RUDY'S 12 LESSONS FOR YOUNG CHAMPIONS

1. Develop your Dream and set realistic goals.

2. Get advice and good information from mentors who believe in your Dream.

3. Listen to good positive music, read positive books, and watch positive movies.

4. Hang out with friends that encourage you, not friends that put you down.

5. Always be a good example for others.

6. Inspire others to be their best.

7. Believe in yourself and take action. Action eliminates fear.

8. Prepare for your Dream, focus, and achieve your goals step by step.

9. Use anger in a positive way, to help you overcome your struggles and do something good.

10. Develop courage, faith, and wisdom and go for your Dream.

11. Have a "YES I CAN" attitude.

12. Never Quit!

Epilogue

On the ledge above Monarch Canyon, the crows were unaware of Rudy's outcome. They were sure that he had fallen to his death. For once, they were speechless.

"Well, you gotta give the little dude credit. He tried," snorted Hacker as he blew his nose into his headband and wiped a tear from his eye.

"What are you sniffling about? Didn't you hate him, Hacker?" questioned the flock.

"Hey, come on, now. I have feelings, too. He was my nestmate, you know," Hacker cried.

"Sssshh. What's that sound?" asked one of the crows.

Beneath them the earth trembled, and deep from within the canyon, the wind howled.

"What? What is it?" The crows huddled together and waited.

The sound was deafening and grew louder.

In the distance, on the highest ledge above Monarch Canyon, Mother Eagle, Rudy's Brothers, and the other eagles had taken shelter from the violent winds. The eagles were clinging to the cliffs for safety when they heard the thundering sound.

WWWWOOSSSHHHH!

Rudy exploded out of the canyon, sending crow feathers and headbands flying.

With each graceful sweep, his WINGS of COURAGE took him higher above the tree line and farther away from the frantic and fluttering crows. Beneath him, his forest friends gathered and watched with joy. Higher and higher he rose, past the highest ledge of the canyon. At that moment Rudy caught the glance of his Mother Eagle. She had a tear in her eye. She realized and understood what her son had been through and what he had become . . . and she was proud!

"Who . . . ? Where did that Wind Dancer come from?" whispered the eagles.

"That's Rudy . . . my son!" Mother Eagle proudly announced.

Just then, Rudy felt the cool, mountain wind currents. They were meant only for those with the heart of an eagle.

Joyfully, he let loose with a shrill "SCHREECCHH," declaring himself to be what he was always meant to be,
AN EAGLE,

AN INSPIRATION TO ALL,

A WIND DANCER!

Discussion Questions

1. What made Hacker change his feelings toward Rudy? How was Hacker different?

2. Why did Mother Eagle have a tear in her eye?

3. By Never Quiting on his Dream, Rudy helped others. What did Rudy teach them?

RUDY'S 12 LESSONS FOR YOUNG CHAMPIONS

1. Develop your Dream and set realistic goals.

2. Get advice and good information from mentors who believe in your Dream.

3. Listen to good positive music, read positive books, and watch positive movies.

4. Hang out with friends that encourage you, not friends that put you down.

5. Always be a good example for others.

6. Inspire others to be their best.

7. Believe in yourself and take action. Action eliminates fear.

8. Prepare for your Dream, focus, and achieve your goals step by step.

9. Use anger in a positive way, to help you overcome your struggles and do something good.

10. Develop courage, faith, and wisdom and go for your Dream.

11. Have a "YES I CAN" attitude.

12. Never Quit!